THIS IS A RECORD OF MY FIRST FIVE YEARS

NAME: _____

RACHAEL HALE

MY LIFE AS A BABY

A FIVE YEAR RECORD

WPL

www.wpl.eu.com

in association with PQ Blackwell

CONTENTS

MY DUE DATE

_____

BEFORE I WAS
BORN MY PARENTS
CALLED ME

_____

_____

_____

_____

WHEN THEY WERE
EXPECTING ME MY
PARENTS FELT

_____

_____

_____

_____

_____

_____

WHAT MY PARENTS
WERE DOING WHEN
MY MOTHER WENT
INTO LABOUR

_____

_____

_____

_____

DATE   _____

TIME   _____

DAY OF WEEK   _____

LENGTH OF LABOUR   _____

LOCATION/HOSPITAL   _____

MEDICAL TEAM   _____

_____

SUPPORT CREW   _____

_____

_____

SPECIAL MEMORIES   _____

_____

_____

_____

_____

YOUR PHOTO HERE

YOUR PHOTO HERE

YOUR PHOTO HERE

YOUR PHOTO HERE

PHOTOGRAPHS

YOUR PHOTO HERE

YOUR PHOTO HERE

YOUR PHOTO HERE

YOUR PHOTO HERE

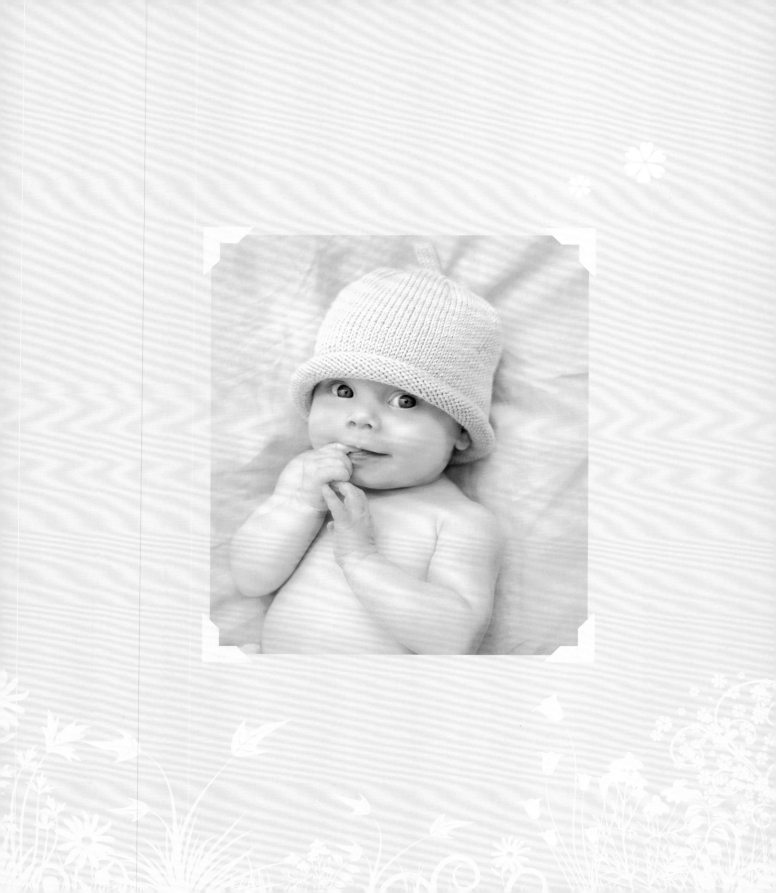

MY WEIGHT

MY LENGTH

MY HAIR COLOUR

MY FIRST MOMENTS
WITH MY PARENTS

A LOCK OF MY
BABY HAIR

MY NAME

MY NAME IS

_____

MY PARENTS
CHOSE IT BECAUSE

_____

_____

MY NICKNAME/S ARE

_____

BECAUSE

_____

OTHER NAMES MY
PARENTS CONSIDERED
WERE

_____

_____

_____

DATE   PLACE

MY NAMING CEREMONY

_____   _____

PERFORMED BY

_____

MY CEREMONY WAS

_____

_____

MY PARENTS' FAVOURITE
MEMORY OF THE DAY

_____

_____

_____

YOUR PHOTO HERE

YOUR PHOTO HERE

YOUR PHOTO HERE

YOUR PHOTO HERE

PHOTOGRAPHS

YOUR PHOTO HERE

YOUR PHOTO HERE

YOUR PHOTO HERE

YOUR PHOTO HERE

WHAT WAS HAPPENING
IN THE WORLD

THE NUMBER-ONE SONG _____

THE NUMBER-ONE FILM _____

A MOVIE TICKET COST _____

ONE LITRE OF MILK COST _____

THE NEWS STORIES OF THE DAY

_____

_____

_____

_____

_____

IMPORTANT LEADERS
AROUND THE WORLD

_____

_____

_____

_____

_____

_____

MY PARENTS FELT

_____

I WENT HOME ON

_____

THE CAR I RODE IN WAS

_____

MY FIRST HOME WAS AT

_____

FAMILY AND FRIENDS
THERE TO WELCOME ME

_____

_____

WHERE I FIRST SLEPT

_____

I SLEPT FOR _____ HOURS

YOUR PHOTO HERE

YOUR PHOTO HERE

FAMILY TREE

| GREAT GRANDPARENTS | GREAT GRANDPARENTS | GREAT GRANDPARENTS | GREAT GRANDPARENTS |

GRANDMOTHER | GRANDFATHER | GRANDMOTHER | GRANDFATHER

AUNTS/UNCLES | MOTHER | FATHER | AUNTS/UNCLES

BROTHERS | ME | SISTERS

YOUR FAMILY PHOTO HERE

YOUR FAMILY PHOTO HERE

YOUR FAMILY PHOTO HERE

YOUR FAMILY PHOTO HERE

FRIENDS & LOVED ONES

YOUR FAMILY PHOTO HERE

YOUR FAMILY PHOTO HERE

YOUR FAMILY PHOTO HERE

YOUR FAMILY PHOTO HERE

IN THE BEGINNING

_____

_____

BEDTIME RITUALS

_____

_____

_____

_____

LULLABIES I LOVE

_____

_____

_____

MY CUTEST
SLEEPING HABIT

_____

_____

_____

	AGE	DATE
IMPORTANT DATES SLEEPING IN A COT		
SLEEPING IN A BED		

MY FAVOURITE
BEDTIME TOY/S

_____

_____

_____

_____

_____

PICTURE

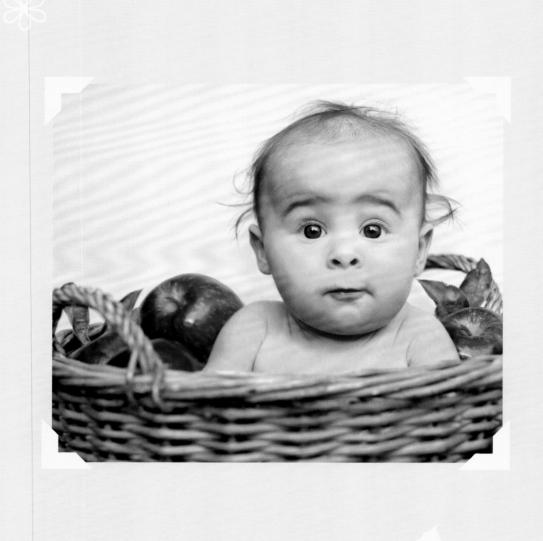

MY APPETITE

FOODS I LIKE

FOODS I DISLIKE

	AGE	DATE
WEANED FROM BREAST/BOTTLE		
MY FIRST TOOTH		
EATING SOLID FOOD		
SITTING IN A HIGHCHAIR		
DRINKING FROM A CUP		

PICTURE

SITTING UP

AGE _____

DATE _____

CRAWLING

AGE _____

DATE _____

WAVING BYE-BYE

AGE _____

DATE _____

STANDING UP

AGE _____

DATE _____

MY FIRST STEPS

AGE _____

DATE _____

FIRST PAIR OF SHOES

AGE _____

DATE _____

SIZE _____

YOUR PHOTO HERE

YOUR PHOTO HERE

YOUR PHOTO HERE

YOUR PHOTO HERE

PHOTOGRAPHS

YOUR PHOTO HERE

YOUR PHOTO HERE

YOUR PHOTO HERE

YOUR PHOTO HERE

MY FIRST WORDS

_____

_____

_____

_____

_____

MY FAVOURITE SAYING

_____

_____

_____

_____

_____

MY FAVOURITE SONG

_____

_____

_____

_____

_____

AGE   DATE

IMPORTANT DATES   COUNTING TO TEN   _____

SINGING THE ALPHABET   _____

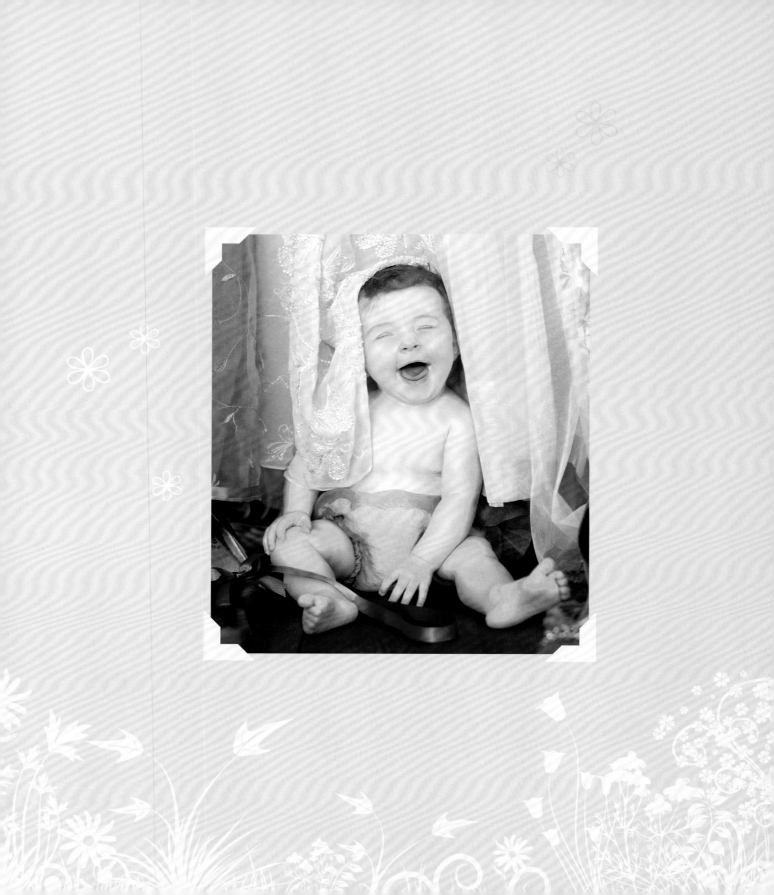

THINGS THAT MAKE ME HAPPY

_____

_____

_____

_____

_____

_____

THINGS THAT MAKE ME SAD

_____

_____

_____

_____

_____

HOW MY PARENTS COMFORT ME

_____

_____

_____

_____

_____

WHEN I WAS HAPPY

YOUR PHOTO HERE

WHEN I WAS SAD

YOUR PHOTO HERE

MY FEELINGS
ABOUT BATH TIME

_____

_____

_____

_____

MY FAVOURITE
BATH TOY/S

_____

_____

_____

_____

WATER GAMES
I LOVE

_____

_____

_____

YOUR PHOTO HERE

YOUR PHOTO HERE

MY FAVOURITE THINGS

GAMES
_____
_____
_____
_____

TOYS
_____
_____
_____

BOOKS
_____
_____
_____

CLOTHES
_____
_____
_____

ACTIVITES
_____
_____
_____

PLACES
_____
_____
_____

DRESS-UPS
_____
_____
_____

TELEVISION CHARACTERS
_____
_____
_____

COLOURS

HOLIDAYS & TRAVEL

MY FIRST HOLIDAY

_____

_____

DATE

_____

WHERE WE WENT

_____

_____

WHO WENT WITH ME

_____

_____

_____

WHAT WE DID

_____

_____

_____

_____

_____

_____

YOUR PHOTO HERE

YOUR PHOTO HERE

YOUR PHOTO HERE

YOUR PHOTO HERE

PHOTOGRAPHS

DATE

EVENT

FAMILY AND FRIENDS
WHO ATTENDED

DATE

EVENT

FAMILY AND FRIENDS
WHO ATTENDED

YOUR PHOTO HERE

YOUR PHOTO HERE

YOUR PHOTO HERE

YOUR PHOTO HERE

PHOTOGRAPHS

YOUR PHOTO HERE

YOUR PHOTO HERE

YOUR PHOTO HERE

YOUR PHOTO HERE

MY CAREGIVER/S NAMES

_____

_____

_____

WHERE THEY LOOK
AFTER ME

_____

_____

_____

GAMES THEY PLAY
WITH ME

_____

_____

_____

_____

PICTURE

MY FAVOURITE THINGS

GAMES

TOYS

BOOKS

ACTIVITIES

CLOTHES

COLOURS

TELEVISION CHARACTERS

PLACES

OTHER

GOING OUT

FUN PLACES WE VISIT

FAVOURITE OUTSIDE ACTIVITIES

SPECIAL OUTINGS WITH GRANDPARENTS/RELATIVES/FRIENDS AND PLAYMATES

YOUR PHOTO HERE

YOUR PHOTO HERE

YOUR PHOTO HERE

YOUR PHOTO HERE

PHOTOGRAPHS

MY FIRST BIRTHDAY PARTY

HOW WE CELEBRATED _____

_____

_____

_____

WHO ATTENDED _____

_____

_____

_____

_____

_____

_____

_____

_____

_____

MY BIRTHDAY CAKE _____

_____

MY FAVOURITE GIFT _____

_____

MY BIRTHDAY CAKE

YOUR PHOTO HERE

MY FAVOURITE GIFT

YOUR PHOTO HERE

MY SECOND YEAR

MY FAVOURITE THINGS

GAMES

TOYS

BOOKS

ACTIVITIES

CLOTHES

COLOURS

TELEVISION CHARACTERS

PLACES

OTHER

GOING OUT

FUN PLACES WE VISIT

FAVOURITE OUTSIDE ACTIVITIES

SPECIAL OUTINGS WITH GRANDPARENTS/RELATIVES/FRIENDS AND PLAYMATES

YOUR PHOTO HERE

YOUR PHOTO HERE

YOUR PHOTO HERE

YOUR PHOTO HERE

PHOTOGRAPHS

HOW WE CELEBRATED

_____

_____

_____

_____

WHO ATTENDED

_____

_____

_____

_____

_____

_____

_____

_____

_____

_____

_____

MY BIRTHDAY CAKE

_____

_____

MY FAVOURITE GIFT

_____

MY BIRTHDAY CAKE

YOUR PHOTO HERE

MY FAVOURITE GIFT

YOUR PHOTO HERE

MY FAVOURITE THINGS

GAMES

TOYS

BOOKS

ACTIVITIES

CLOTHES

COLOURS

TELEVISION CHARACTERS

PLACES

OTHER

GOING OUT

FUN PLACES WE VISIT

FAVOURITE OUTSIDE ACTIVITIES

SPECIAL OUTINGS WITH GRANDPARENTS/RELATIVES/FRIENDS AND PLAYMATES

YOUR PHOTO HERE

YOUR PHOTO HERE

YOUR PHOTO HERE

YOUR PHOTO HERE

MY THIRD BIRTHDAY PARTY

HOW WE CELEBRATED _____

_____

_____

_____

WHO ATTENDED _____

_____

_____

_____

_____

_____

_____

_____

_____

_____

MY BIRTHDAY CAKE _____

_____

_____

MY FAVOURITE GIFT _____

_____

MY BIRTHDAY CAKE

YOUR PHOTO HERE

MY FAVOURITE GIFT

YOUR PHOTO HERE

MY FAVOURITE THINGS

GAMES _____

TOYS _____

BOOKS _____

ACTIVITIES _____

CLOTHES _____

COLOURS _____

TELEVISION CHARACTERS _____

PLACES _____

OTHER _____

_____

GOING OUT

FUN PLACES WE VISIT _____

_____

FAVOURITE OUTSIDE ACTIVITIES _____

_____

SPECIAL OUTINGS WITH GRANDPARENTS/RELATIVES/FRIENDS AND PLAYMATES _____

_____

_____

_____

YOUR PHOTO HERE

YOUR PHOTO HERE

YOUR PHOTO HERE

YOUR PHOTO HERE

PHOTOGRAPHS

MY FOURTH BIRTHDAY PARTY

HOW WE CELEBRATED
_____
_____
_____
_____

WHO ATTENDED
_____
_____
_____
_____
_____
_____
_____
_____
_____

MY BIRTHDAY CAKE
_____
_____

MY FAVOURITE GIFT
_____
_____

MY BIRTHDAY CAKE

YOUR PHOTO HERE

MY FAVOURITE GIFT

YOUR PHOTO HERE

MY FIFTH YEAR

MY FAVOURITE THINGS

GAMES

TOYS

BOOKS

ACTIVITIES

CLOTHES

COLOURS

TELEVISION CHARACTERS

PLACES

OTHER

GOING OUT

FUN PLACES WE VISIT

FAVOURITE OUTSIDE ACTIVITIES

SPECIAL OUTINGS WITH GRANDPARENTS/RELATIVES/FRIENDS AND PLAYMATES

YOUR PHOTO HERE

YOUR PHOTO HERE

YOUR PHOTO HERE

YOUR PHOTO HERE

PHOTOGRAPHS

MY FIFTH BIRTHDAY PARTY

HOW WE CELEBRATED
_____

_____

_____

_____

WHO ATTENDED
_____

_____

_____

_____

_____

_____

_____

_____

_____

_____

MY BIRTHDAY CAKE
_____

_____

MY FAVOURITE GIFT
_____

_____

MY BIRTHDAY CAKE

YOUR PHOTO HERE

MY FAVOURITE GIFT

YOUR PHOTO HERE

HAND & FOOT PRINTS

IN THE BEGINNING

DATE _____

HAND

FOOT

HAND & FOOT PRINTS

AT AGE FIVE

DATE _____

HAND

FOOT

HEALTH

BLOOD TYPE

_____

ALLERGIES

_____

_____

_____

_____

IMMUNISATION	AGE	DATE

ILLNESSES	AGE	DATE

GROWTH

HEIGHT

BORN

3MTHS

6MTHS

9MTHS

1YR

2YR

3YR

4YR

5YR

MY HEIGHT CHART

WEIGHT

BORN

3MTHS

6MTHS

9MTHS

1YR

2YR

3YR

4YR

5YR

MY WEIGHT CHART

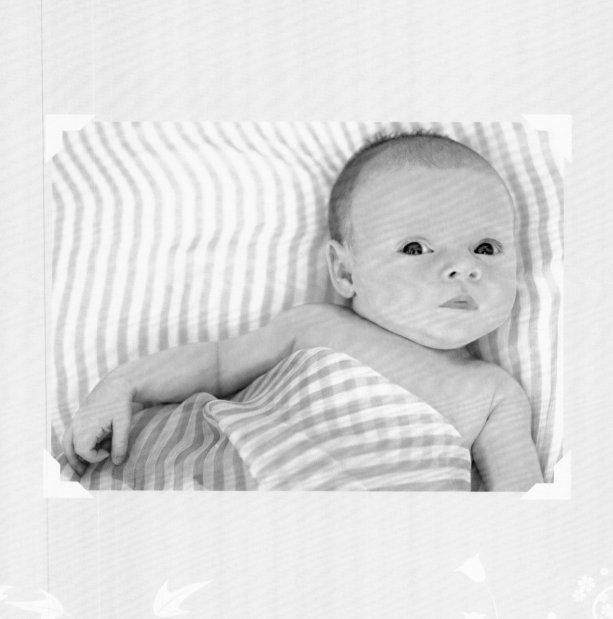

MY PARENTS' SPECIAL
MESSAGE FOR ME

DATE

DATE

MY FIRST TOOTH

MY FIRST TOOTHBRUSH

MY FIRST BED

MY FIRST NIGHT AWAY FROM HOME

MY FIRST WORD

MY FIRST STEP

MY FIRST DAY AT PRESCHOOL

MY FIRST DAY AT SCHOOL

MY FIRST SHOES

I WAS   OLD

THEY WERE SIZE

MY FIRST HAIRCUT

I WAS   OLD

CUT BY

MY FIRST FRIEND

MY FIRST PET

MY FIRST BICYCLE

YOUR PHOTO HERE

YOUR PHOTO HERE

www.wpl.eu.com

The Perfume Factory
140 Wales Farm Road
London, W3 6UG, UK

ISBN: 978-1-904264-52-1

This edition produced and originated by PQ Blackwell Limited,
116 Symonds Street, Auckland, New Zealand
www.pqblackwell.com

This edition published in 2008 exclusively by WPL. www.wpl.eu.com

Printed in China by 1010 Printing International Ltd.